AFRICAN-AMERICAN ARTS

Music

Angela Shelf Medearis and
Michael R. Medearis

Twenty-First Century Books
A Division of Henry Holt and Company • New York

Twenty-First Century Books
A Division of Henry Holt and Company, Inc.
115 West 18th Street
New York, NY 10011

Library of Congress Cataloging-in-Publication Data
Medearis, Angela Shelf, 1956–
Music / Angela S. Medearis, Michael R. Medearis.
p. cm.—(African-American arts)
Summary: Discusses the evolution of African-American music from
its roots in the rhythms and instruments from Africa through the development
of the blues, gospel, and soul to modern rock and rap.
1. Afro-Americans—Music—History and criticism—Juvenile literature. 2. Popular music—United
States—History and criticism—Juvenile literature. [1. Afro-Americans—Music. 2. Popular music—
History and criticism.] I. Medearis, Michael. II. Title. III. Series.
ML3479.M43 1997
780'.89'96073—dc21

96-47276
CIP
AC MN

ISBN 0-8050-4482-5
First Edition—1997

DESIGNED BY KELLY SOONG

Printed in the United States of America
All first editions are printed on acid-free paper. ∞

1 3 5 7 9 10 8 6 4 2

Photo Credits

p. 4 (top): ©Xavier Rossi/Gamma Liaison; p. 4 (bottom): ©M. Amon/Tony Stone Images; pp. 8, 24 (left
and middle), 28, 36: Peter Newark's American Pictures; pp. 11, 39, 58, 68: Archive Photos; pp. 14, 27:
The Granger Collection; pp. 19 (both), 25 (middle), 35, 69: Corbis-Bettmann; pp. 24 (right), 25 (left),
53, 62: Archive Photos/Frank Driggs Collection; pp. 25 (right), 44, 51, 67: Photofest; p. 31: ©Richard
Braaten/Kennedy Center; pp. 40, 47: UPI/Corbis-Bettmann; p. 42: ©Reuters/Greta Pratt/Archive
Photos; pp. 54, 70 (bottom): Reuters/Corbis-Bettmann; p. 70 (top): ©Reuters/Str. Marcos
Pacheco/Archive Photos; p. 74: ©Raymond Boyd/Michael Ochs Archives/Venice, CA; p. 77: ©Sheila
Turner.

CONTENTS

The heritage continues...

INTRODUCTION

In ancient African times, when the sun rose over the horizon, you could hear the sound of drums. In Africa the drum was used not only for entertainment, but also as another way for people to talk. Because the drums sounded like people speaking, they were called talking drums.

In Nigeria drums called *dundun* were used. A group of three to five drummers would play several types of *dundun* drums. First there was the *iya ilu*, which was the big "mother drum." The *kerikeri* and the *gangan* were medium-sized drums. There was the small round *gudugudu* and finally the very small *kanango*. All of the drums other than the *gudugudu* had a long wooden body with bowl-shaped ends. The drums were made by stretching animal hides over hollowed-out logs. Squeezing and releasing the leather strings attached to the hides made the drums sound higher or lower.

African drumming is made up of a number of different rhythms. Each drummer takes the beat and weaves it into a crisscross pattern of sound. The highly skilled African drummers had a way of striking their drums with a curved drumstick so that each one made its own special sound. The high and low sounds of the voice in African speech could be imitated this way. Talking drums were used to spread messages throughout many parts of Africa. Everyone in the village understood the sound of the drums, just as if they were speaking. Drums were especially important in the palaces of African kings. They were played at festivals, funerals, and joyful times of worship, prayer, and praise. Sometimes the rhythm of the drum made the listeners want to move and to dance. The drums sometimes spoke about ancient ancestors. One drum message talked about past warrior chiefs who fought bravely, and others gave honor to the present chief of the village. This is what the drums said:

Child of death,
Father of all mothers,
King of all kings.
You carry the blackness of the forest
Like a royal gown.
You carry the blood of your enemies
Like a shining crown.

In West Africa songs were used to communicate many different kinds of messages. They were also an important part of the celebration of special occasions. Songs were sung to mark a memorable event such as a baby's birth or the death of a relative. Songs were also used to teach children the proper way to act.

Today each of the West African countries of Senegal, Gambia, Liberia, the Ivory Coast, Ghana, Guinea, and Nigeria has its own special style of music. The oldest and most important musical instrument used in Africa is the drum.

The use of talking drums was one of several ancient musical traditions that traveled from Africa to America. Although the sounds of the drum were first heard thousands of years ago, the drum continues to be an important tie between African and African-American music.

THE AFRICAN CONNECTION

Over three hundred years ago, when West African captives were forced into slavery in the Americas, they brought with them a strong sense of their cultural heritage and their music. The complex, multipatterned rhythms of African drumming, although not used directly in African-American music, are still a large influence. These rhythm patterns were fused with European harmonies to bring forth a unique American sound. This rhythmic blend continues to be the common link between African and African-American music.

Although the drum plays an important role in African music, this was not the only instrument Africans developed. A variety of musical instruments have been produced and played in Africa for hundreds of years, including bells, gongs, xylophones, thumb pianos, harps, horns, flutes, lutes, and fiddles. The modern banjo is based on a stringed instrument that originally came from Africa.

African musical skill was recognized over 2,000 years ago by Hanno, an ancient sea captain from Carthage (in what is now Tunisia). He visited the

West African coast and saw many different instruments being played. European traders sailing to West Africa in the early 1600s were also amazed by the music.

In 1817 Edward Bowdich was sent by the African Committee of London to trade with the Ashanti people of Ghana in West Africa. Bowdich was an amateur musician who wrote detailed notes describing the instruments he saw and the music he heard. The music used intricate melodies that seemed to be made up by the performers as it was being played. What Bowdich experienced was a quality of African music called improvisation. He also heard drummers beating out a series of complex multiple rhythms that sounded very difficult to play. The African musical traits of improvisation and multiple rhythms are major links to modern music that are especially evident in jazz but can also be heard in many other forms of African-American music.

The slave trade spread throughout the Americas, along with the music of the West African captives. The captives were taken by ship to several places in the New World. During the trip they were often brought up on

African captives being loaded into the hold of a ship headed for the New World

deck for exercise where they were then forced to sing and dance in the open air to entertain the crew.

In the early 1800s a slave ship captain named Theodore Canot described how the captives kept their music alive as they were brought to the New World: "During afternoons of serene weather, men, women, girls and boys are allowed while on deck to unite in African melodies which they always enhance [make better] by extemporaneous [unrehearsed] tom-tom [drum] on the bottom of a tub or tin kettle."

African captives could not always talk to one another because they were taken from tribes all over Africa and most of them spoke different languages. The slave ship captains felt that if the slaves could talk to one another they might take over the ship, so they mixed people from different tribes together. However, the Africans could talk with one another through their music. They used the rhythms of their crude drums to send messages. For example, certain drumbeats were a signal for the slaves to rebel. Between 1699 and 1845 there were at least fifty-five revolts aboard slave ships.

The African captives could not bring anything from their homelands. The memories of their former way of life were all they had. Fortunately many held on to the rich musical traditions that were such an important part of their lives in Africa. White Americans did not understand or accept the African sense of rhythm and musical expression. According to the European standards most Americans were used to, African music was culturally inferior. African musical forms were often referred to as "primitive."

In the New World a number of American slaveholders discouraged their African captives from singing or dancing in the traditional ways of their former homelands. This forced the Africans to disguise their ancient cultural traditions behind new forms of music and dance that were more acceptable. The slaves borrowed European musical traits and combined them with African musical traditions, producing a new kind of music. They also found materials in the Americas to make new musical instruments similar to the ones they had in Africa.

For some time slave owners did not know that the captives were using drums to talk to one another. They thought that the slaves were only making music to help them do hard work on the plantation. Actually a drummer could beat out a message on the drum in a kind of code.

When the slave owners outlawed the use of drums, the slaves made drum rhythms by stomping their feet on the floors of their huts or on boards. Using feet to sound out a rhythm was also common in some parts of Africa. A number of revolts or escapes were started when the slaves tapped their heels in a secret code on wood floors.

Often slaves were not allowed to talk to one another while working in the fields, so they used "calls" to talk. Calls were an attempt to change speech into song. Short messages were sung to attract attention; to warn other workers that the white overseer was coming; to call the slaves to work, to eat, or to gather. When slavery was abolished and more blacks moved to the cities, the use of calls became less common.

It is certain that these calls were sung in African dialects during the early part of African-American history. In Africa people commonly called one another with songlike messages. These messages could announce a village emergency, gather a work group, or extend personal greetings to a neighbor. Calls could be heard from great distances and in America were better known as "hollers." The slaves at work in the fields used field hollers.

Slaves sang with distinctive African overtones. The rhythmic chanting of black work songs goes back thousands of years to ancient African cultural practices of singing while working. In sub-Saharan Africa people have always sung while working. In America, this tradition served the plantation owners well, as they noticed that the slaves worked harder as they sang. Some songs were about picking cotton, while other songs told about working on the docks loading and unloading ships.

The subject of the work songs depended on the labor being done and how the slaves felt at the time. There were work songs on the railroad, fishing boats, and plantations. Sounds, such as an ax chopping wood or the pounding of grain in a mortar, often added rhythm to the song. The rattle of chains in prison camps provided background rhythms for work songs. Black prisoners sang about unfair treatment, troubles with the law, prison life, women, love, and other subjects that reflected their lives. Such subjects could be heard in the words of later blues songs.

Most slave owners believed that slaves who were converted to Christianity would not want to revolt. Many slaves accepted Christianity. In their religious services they sang beautiful music that expressed their feelings about God and their newfound faith. Music from African traditions and American slave cultures was blended with the traditional English hymns of American Protestants to produce black spirituals.

For many years spirituals were called sorrow songs because they were mostly about the suffering of black people and their hope for a peaceable kingdom in heaven. The slaves also concealed messages in their spirituals. They were used to plan meetings, to help escaped slaves, and to remind one another of the hope for freedom. A spiritual called "Deep River," for example, was used to tell other slaves of a meeting by the river:

Spirituals were an important part of the slaves' prayer meetings. Many of the meetings were not allowed by the slave owners and had to be held in secret.

Deep river
My home is over Jordan, yes
Deep river, Lord
I want to cross over into camp ground.

Sometimes a slave would run away. When the master discovered that a slave had escaped, the other slaves would sing the spiritual "Wade in the Water." The slaves on the other plantations would hear the song and sing it. The runaway would then know to go to the river, where the bloodhounds used to track escaped slaves could not follow the scent.

The Underground Railroad was the route that runaway slaves traveled north to freedom. It was made up of a group of homes and hiding places. Many whites and free blacks would hide runaways because they did not believe slavery was right. Each house represented a "station" where runaways would stop to rest and get food and clothing. The free blacks would sing a spiritual called "The Gospel Train" to let the runaways know when to move to the next station. This would continue from station to station until the journey was over:

The Gospel train is coming.
I hear it just at hand—
I hear the car wheels moving,
And rumbling thro' the land.
Get on board—children, children.
Get on board—children, children.
Get on board—children, children.
There's room for many a more.

Group call-and-response singing is a common African musical form. Many of the songs are composed of short, often-repeated musical phrases and longer improvisational phrases that are never repeated in the same form. One type of call-and-response found in sub-Saharan African cultures involves two musicians who sing a song as if they are talking to each other. Vocal interplay between a lead singer and a responding chorus is another example.

The call-and-response singing style allowed a leader to make up the words for new verses of the songs and then be answered by a group. The slaves would sing spirituals in this way during church services. The call-and-response style of singing was very useful when only a few people were able to read the hymnal. Field hollers and other early black work songs also used the call-and-response form of singing.

There were a number of features of European music that were familiar to the slaves in spite of the differences in rhythm, performance style, and harmony. American Protestant churches of the mid-seventeenth century used revival songs, camp-meeting songs, and hymns. This music came from the "lining out" of words from the book of Psalms in the Bible. A leader would read aloud (line out) the words from the psalm text, one line at a time, for the people in the congregation who could not read. After each line was read, the congregation would follow in singing that line to a familiar melody. This style of singing that African captives encountered is comparable to the ancient African call-and-response musical tradition.

One group in particular helped to popularize spirituals. On January 9, 1866, the Freedmen's Bureau of the federal government founded Fisk University in Nashville, Tennessee, to help educate the newly freed slaves. The Freedmen's Bureau gave the school only enough money to get started, but not enough to keep it going.

The American Missionary Society helped the school by providing an abandoned hospital barracks that it bought in 1865 to use for classrooms. This became the first building of the new school. Unfortunately no heat was in the building and there was no food for the students. Frustrated that the school would not be able to operate under these conditions, the society talked about closing it. The Reverend George L. White, the music director at Fisk University, did not want to see the school closed. He thought of a plan to help keep it open.

In 1871 nine young black singers left Fisk University to raise money for the school. Except for one of them, all were recently freed slaves. The year of Emancipation was called "jubilee" by black people, so the students named their group the Fisk Jubilee Singers in memory of that time.

The Fisk Jubilee Singers started out singing current popular songs. Later, Director White encouraged them to sing spirituals. The group first performed a selection of spirituals at a meeting of the National Council of Congregational Churches held at Oberlin College in 1875. The Fisk Jubilee Singers soon became so popular that after eight months of touring they raised $20,000. Ella Sheppard, a member of the group, wrote, "After many months we began to appreciate the wonderful beauty and power of

The Fisk Jubilee Singers in 1880

our songs; but continued to sing in public the usual choruses, duets, solos, etc. Occasionally two or three slave songs were sung at the close of the concert. But the demand of the public changed this order. Soon the land rang with our slave songs."

The Fisk Jubilee Singers performed all over the United States and Europe. After finishing their second European tour, they were recognized by European and American composers as bringing forth the most exciting and original elements of black music. This music was considered to be one of the purest forms of American folk music. The Czech composer Antonín Dvořák used African-American spirituals to describe America in his symphony *From the New World* in 1893.

Spirituals from black churches have greatly affected the development of American music. Many popular black singers and musicians began their careers performing in black churches.

Music was an important part of African life. The captives cherished the songs and rhythms they were able to pass on from their heritage. The music that was brought from Africa was changed by the experiences of slavery, but it kept many of its original traits. Western European music also affected the music of the African captives. The African-American folk music produced by this mixture was the first music to be "discovered" and revealed to Americans and the world as the true folk music of the United States. The African captives' experiences were often expressed in a musical form that later came to be known as the blues.

THE BLUES
EXPERIENCE

No one knows exactly where the blues started, but it is generally agreed that the strongest influences came from the work songs sung by slaves in the South. Blues singing developed from the call-and-response form of field hollers and other early black work songs that were commonly sung in many parts of Africa. The blues style is a combination of many types of black folk music, including African chants and spirituals. Spirituals are based on religious beliefs and a better life after death, while the blues are rooted in the joys and struggles of everyday life.

As one listens carefully to different blues songs, the music does not necessarily sound sad or depressing. Blues singers can perform their songs with a soulful quality that deeply reflects emotions difficult to express in words alone. Although the words frequently deal with misfortune and loss, the blues combine feelings of misery with a sense of hopeful optimism. The bold sounds of the accompanying guitar, piano, or other instruments have an uplifting effect in contrast to the sorrow of the lyrics. The shared experiences of many generations of African Americans are reflected in the messages found in the blues. The anger, sadness, pain, and determination expressed by the blues singer give the song its power.

In the most common type of blues, one line is sung and then repeated. Then a different line is sung. The repetition creates a sense of drama, and the third line delivers the punch. The accompanying instruments fill out the music to develop a call-and-response pattern between the voice and the instruments. A typical blues song might look like the following:

> *I'm goin' down to the station, 'cause I'm leavin' this town.*
> *I'm goin' down to the station, 'cause I'm leavin' this town.*
> *Since my baby done left me, ain't no use in hangin' roun'.*

The playing and singing of the blues involves the use of what are called blue notes. These notes are flatted or "bent" to change the key from major to minor, giving the music a mournful quality. The blue notes came from a different musical scale that was common in Africa but generally unknown in Europe and the New World. This scale produced notes in which the third (E in the key of C), or mediant, and the seventh (B in the key of C), or leading tone, were flattened. Blue notes became the basis of a musical language that eventually emerged as jazz.

In African tradition it is difficult to separate religious thought from daily life experiences. The idea that music can express the feelings of people dealing with their many day-to-day struggles is a major part of the blues. When B. B. King does an especially moving concert of "down-home blues," his powerful delivery of a song moves the audience much like an old black spiritual. Along with spirituals, the blues were also influenced by the strong feelings generated by the field hollers of black slaves.

Just as different aspects of the spirituals can be heard in the blues, the blues also influenced other musical styles. The basic blues rhythm directly reflects the African use of complex rhythms. The African-derived beat gave the music a "swinging" effect.

The man who called himself the Father of the Blues came from a strict religious background. William Christopher (W. C.) Handy was born of two generations of black Methodist ministers. His parents and his grandfather believed that musical expression should be limited to singing and playing hymns in church. But the African tradition of making and enjoying music for everyday life proved to have a stronger influence on Handy.

Handy grew up with a love for different types of music. As a child he would sneak away to hear the songs of the black laborers working along the Tennessee River. Handy also taught himself to play the cornet. In 1893 he formed a quartet that was featured at the World's Columbian Exposition in Chicago. His group was one of the most sought-after bands in the country, but broke up because of money problems. He then became band director and solo cornetist of Mahara's Colored Minstrels.

During a California performance in 1897 Handy decided to play a composition that reflected the black work songs and spirituals he had heard as a child. This song, "Georgia Camp Meeting," was so well received that Handy decided to form another band to play it.

People enjoyed the music of Handy's band because it was easy to dance to. Although the band was very successful, an event took place that would greatly change Handy's musical direction. In Cleveland the band was challenged to a music contest by an unimpressive-looking group made up of three musicians. One of them played guitar, and the others played mandolin and bass violin. This group played music that sounded like a "backyard wail," yet it was different and exciting. The other band easily won the contest. Handy then realized that the music he really wanted to play would have to express the feelings of black people growing up in America.

Handy began searching for music with roots in black folklife. He went to saloons to hear what black people talked about. He hung around the railroad yards and the docks and listened closely to the sorrowful songs of black people. Here he developed his version of the blues. Common people

W. C. Handy and a young Dinah Shore rehearsing for a radio broadcast.
The inset shows the 1914 cover of Handy's "Saint Louis Blues"
music, which was the first successful blues ever published.

could identify with the subjects of Handy's songs. Each song seemed to tell a story about the person singing it.

Handy saw that the instrument used most often with these blues songs was the guitar. Guitarlike one-stringed instruments were common in West Africa. The guitar's appeal to blacks, and the skill with which they played it, can be traced to similar sounding string instruments in Africa.

The sheet music for "The Memphis Blues" was published by Handy in 1912 and written in "tango rhythm." The tango rhythm began in Africa, where it was called *tangana*. Handy's tango music was usually recognized as having come from Spain, but many music historians believe that the Spanish obtained it from Africa during the slave trade. The tango rhythm is the foundation for most Afro-Caribbean music. It is also the folk music of Brazil, which has a large number of African descendants. It is not known how Handy found these rhythms, but the African rhythms he used show how blues is linked to its African roots. Although he was not a blues singer, Handy was the first person to publish blues songs. Later he would write "St. Louis Blues," which is probably his most famous blues song.

The typical blues performer would often hum as he played his tune. He might even sing in a high-pitched voice or a low moan to give the listener a sense of the song's feelings of sadness. Sometimes rhythmic chanting techniques like those used by preachers in black churches would be used.

The blues are usually described under one of two categories: rural (usually called country) blues and urban (or city) blues. The country blues were closer to the field hollers and shouts of the spirituals. Early country blues singers were black men in the rural South from the states of Mississippi, Louisiana, and Texas who sang folktales about everyday life and lost lovers. The instrument of choice for country blues was the bottleneck guitar, but the singer was sometimes accompanied by a jaw harp or harmonica. Country blues singers would often use improvisation in their songs.

The Mississippi Delta region was home to some of the most famous country blues singers. Some influential early blues singers from this area are

Charlie Patton, Son House, and Robert Johnson. Patton is recognized as the founder of the Delta blues and in 1929 was one of the first Mississippi bluesmen to record. House was famous for his use of bottleneck guitar. Johnson changed blues history as the first known guitar player to use the walking bass line of boogie-woogie. This style involved putting extra emphasis on the rhythm and was the basis for the Chicago blues.

John Lee Hooker was another country blues great from the Mississippi Delta. Hooker, who played professionally in the South until 1948, was known for his extraordinary rhythmic sense and a voice that could deliver deeply expressive music. He moved North and continued performing his brand of country blues well into the 1990s. Hooker once said of the blues, "It's not only what happened to you . . . it's what happened to your fore-parents and other people. And that's what makes the blues."

Big Bill Broonzy was gifted with a powerful voice and delivered his blues in the vocal style of a gospel singer. Broonzy's innovative performances dominated the blues up until World War II. He toured Europe from 1951 to 1958, and created for himself the title of "the last blues singer alive." He used his influence to help other artists record.

Muddy Waters (Mckinley Morganfield) was a central figure in the history of the blues and was also responsible for creating much of the music known as Chicago blues. Bukka White was considered a master of the Delta blues. He is said to have given his cousin, the now famous B. B. King, his first guitar.

Texas country blues singers developed a style that was a little different from that of Mississippi blues singers. It used fewer chords, was more vocal, and put emphasis on the melody, which would be played on a single guitar string during breaks in the song. Blind Lemon Jefferson and Texas Alexander were founders of this unique sound. Lightnin' Hopkins developed his own style of Texas blues and recorded up until 1966. Mance Lipscomb was a Texas blues singer who performed well into his sixties. His soft approach to the blues set him apart from other Texas blues artists.

Huddie "Leadbelly" Ledbetter was a country blues artist from the South whose incredible musical abilities helped obtain international recognition for the blues. Born in Louisiana but raised in Texas, his popularity as a singer kept him traveling between both states. Unfortunately Leadbelly's fast lifestyle landed him in prison for murder. His singing in prison so impressed the authorities that, with the help of white folklorist Alan Lomax, he was able to get a pardon. Leadbelly became Lomax's chauffeur and helped him collect songs all over the South.

Leadbelly was a versatile performer who used a variety of styles including folk music, cowboy songs, and lullabies. In 1934 he was the first black from the South to sing for a white audience in New York, where he attracted the attention of white folk music legends Woody Guthrie and Pete Seeger. After World War II, he toured France and opened the way for future bluesmen to play in Europe. Leadbelly composed his most famous song, "Goodnight, Irene," in 1949, the year of his death. Leadbelly's contributions to black popular music greatly influenced many younger musicians.

The southeastern section of the United States also produced a number of popular blues artists. Most of them took their music to New York, where it received wide acceptance. Brownie McGhee and harmonica player Sonny Terry performed the blues together for over thirty years and were probably the most famous city blues singers of the 1960s. McGhee's musical inspiration was Blind Boy Fuller. Fuller, along with Blind Willie McTell, Blind Blake, and Peg Leg Howell, were from Georgia and the Carolinas. Fuller and Terry played together until Fuller died, then Terry began working with McGhee in New York.

City blues are sometimes called classic blues and are considered to be a more refined and smoother version of country blues. How well these blues are played depends on how the singer improvises on the melody, delivers the vocals, and expresses the sounds of the blue notes in the song. Country blues painted a picture of the harsh life of blacks in the South. Classic blues reflect the experiences of blacks in urban areas.

The blues were very popular during what is called the classic period, from the 1920s until the time of the Great Depression in the 1930s. When phonograph records became easy to make and to buy in the 1930s, blues singers sold millions of records.

Unlike country blues singers, the most important classic blues singers were women. The popularity of women singers in the early minstrel shows and later in vaudeville shows may have been part of the reason for this. Gertrude "Ma" Rainey originated a unique classic blues technique and was later called the Mother of the Blues. Rainey was born Gertrude Pridgett in Georgia in 1886. She was the daughter of minstrel show parents.

Rainey began singing on the stage when she was fourteen. She got her nickname "Ma" after she married William "Pa" Rainey, who was also a minstrel show performer. Gertrude began touring with him in a song-and-dance routine. She had over twenty years of performing experience in traveling circuses and in a variety of minstrel shows before she made her first blues recording. "Countin' the Blues" is an example of a classic blues song by Ma Rainey:

(first of five verses)
Layin' in my bed
with my face turned to the wall.
Lawd, layin' in my bed
with my face turned to the wall.
Tryin' to count those blues
So I could sing them all.

Ma Rainey did not perform outside of the South until 1924. She made several recordings in Chicago and New York up until 1928. By this time, Ma Rainey was said by some to be losing popularity. It was during this four-year period, however, that she recorded with leading jazz musicians Louis Armstrong and Fletcher Henderson. She was also the teacher of the famous blues singer Bessie Smith.

Six famous blues singers (left to right)*: "Leadbelly" Ledbetter, Muddy Waters,*
Blind Lemon Jefferson, Ma Rainey, Bessie Smith, Alberta Hunter

Bessie Smith was born in Chattanooga, Tennessee. She was fourteen years younger than Ma Rainey, but they began recording about the same time. Smith became better known, and many felt that she was a more talented singer. It was the 1920 recording of Bessie Smith's "Crazy Blues" that blazed the trail for the blues. It sold over 790,000 records in the first year that it was released. Smith became so successful that she earned the title Empress of the Blues.

There was a close association between blues performers and jazz musicians. Like Ma Rainey, many of Bessie Smith's songs were made with some of the best jazz artists of the day, such as Clarence Williams, Fletcher Henderson, James P. Johnson, and Louis Armstrong. There were also several other popular women blues singers during the twenties and thirties, among them Alberta Hunter, Bertha Hill, Victoria Spivey, and Ida Cox. By the time that Smith made her last recordings in 1933, her classic blues had, like Ma Rainey's earlier ones, gone out of style. The major blues singers from then on would be men.

The blues had traces of its country roots mixed in with city elements up until the beginning of World War II. The most important change in the blues band would take place in the 1930s with the introduction of the electric guitar. Aaron "T-Bone" Walker was a singer and guitar player from Texas. Before moving to California, Walker had used an electric guitar with his blues singing. Many younger players adopted his style.

Modern blues singers perform mostly in the classic style. Among people that enjoy listening to the blues, B. B. King is the most widely known artist in modern times. It seems appropriate that his last name also describes his position in blues music today.

The quality that separates the blues from other forms of African-American musical expression is its emphasis on the message coming from the personal life of one individual. Blues music deals with subjects that are common to the human experience. The songs express many emotions. This is what gives the blues a universal appeal.

THREE

MINSTREL SHOWS AND RAGTIME

On the evening of February 6, 1843, a new kind of entertainment came to the Bowery Theater on Manhattan's Lower East Side. Four white performers calling themselves the Virginia Minstrels put on blackface makeup as part of a circus act. With blackened faces and lips outlined in white, they sang to the sounds of the banjo, violin, bone castanets, and tambourine in their rendition of a "Negro concert." This performance marked the birth of minstrelsy and the popular minstrel show.

All of the members of the Virginia Minstrels had made stage appearances as individual acts doing characters in blackface before their Bowery Theater debut. It was not the portrayal of black characters that made their February 6 presentation special. It was the fact that this was the first time that a show had been put together based on a format that gave white audiences a picture of plantation life. The minstrel show brought music, comic sketches, and dancing together for a complete variety show that would dominate American entertainment for over half a century.

The musical tradition of working in blackface began in England's music-hall performances of the late 1700s and came to the United States with British immigrants. During the early 1800s several Americans were doing impersonations of Negroes on the stage. Most notable among these were George Washington Dixon and Thomas Dartmouth "Daddy" Rice. Blacks were portrayed on the stage by Dixon as early as 1827 in Albany, New York. In 1829 Dixon performed in blackface at the same Bowery Theater where the Virginia Minstrels would appear sixteen years later.

Dixon portrayed a character named Zip Coon, a Negro city dandy who was always dressed in a high-fashion swallow-tailed coat. Rice played the part of Jim Crow, the plantation slave. Zip Coon is described in Dixon's song that became a minstrel favorite, "Long Tail Blues." Daddy Rice is said to have created the Jim Crow song-and-dance routine after seeing a lame black stable hand perform an unusual limplike dance step as he worked and sang:

"Turn about an' wheel about an' do jes so
An' ebery time I turn about, I jump Jim Crow."

Zip Coon and Jim Crow became two regular characters of the minstrel show. Daddy Rice was an instant hit when he appeared in blackface and tattered clothes, introducing his Jim Crow routine for the first time at the Bowery Theater in 1832. His fame for this performance spread to city after city in America and also led to an outstanding tour of England in 1836. Daddy Rice became known as the father of American minstrelsy.

This 1835 song sheet cover shows "Daddy" Rice in his Jim Crow minstrel performance.

At the time there seemed to be a general admiration by white people of the rhythms and humor shown by blacks. After the Civil War, however, minstrelsy made many changes. White Southerners were bitter about losing their former slaves. They used minstrelsy to show black people as inferior and without morals. These harsh images were offensive to African Americans but were generally accepted by many white people.

The minstrel show was popular from 1843 to 1909, a period lasting over sixty years. The public was so accustomed to the minstrel style that it expected all musicians who played in saloons and cabarets to perform that way. In America black minstrels had to wear the same blackface makeup as the white minstrels to be publicly accepted. Black musicians continued performing this music, although many of them felt it had become too "tired and stiff."

Stephen Foster was a Northern white songwriter who wrote about life in the South before the Civil War. The music he wrote came from black folk songs that he had heard. His songs included "Old Black Joe," "Old Folks At Home" (known also as "Swannee River"), "My Old Kentucky Home," and "Way Down South."

An 1880s poster advertising a minstrel show

Foster said he wanted to be "the best Ethiopian songwriter." This meant he wanted to write the best black minstrel songs. Foster attended minstrel shows and visited Kentucky plantations in 1852 to hear "real Negro plantation singing." His songs described a picture of peaceful plantations and happy black slaves. He was one of the first people to make African American folk music popular.

James Bland was a Northern black songwriter who was not as well known as Stephen Foster. In 1875 he joined a minstrel group called the Original Black Diamonds. Bland wrote much of the new music that was used by both black and white minstrel shows. George Primrose was the greatest white promoter of minstrel shows. When he used some of Bland's songs in his shows, Bland became very famous, particularly for his sentimental songs about the Old South.

Jack Haverly was a white promoter who decided he would use real blacks in his minstrel shows instead of whites in blackface. His group opened in London, England, in 1881 as Haverly's European Minstrels. The hit of the show was James Bland, who performed one of his most famous songs, "O Dem Golden Slippers."

Bland performed for almost ten years in some of the best music halls in Europe without having to use blackface makeup. He returned to America in the early 1900s and found that minstrel shows had been replaced by a new entertainment called vaudeville. After failing to make a comeback in Philadelphia, Bland soon went bankrupt. Although he wrote more than 600 songs, he died penniless and with very little recognition. When Bland was twenty-four years old, he wrote "Carry Me Back to Old Virginia," which became the official state song of Virginia in 1940. Most people thought that it was written by Stephen Foster and were surprised to learn that it was written by a black man.

Both Foster and Bland used elements of African-American folk music—work songs and spirituals. These composers and others changed the black dialect and African-based rhythms to make the songs more acceptable to white audiences. Unfortunately this change left out many of the things that made the music so unique.

Ragtime music sprang up toward the end of the 1800s. Some considered it a style of black music weak in African influence. Others thought it was a direct transfer of African banjo playing to the piano. The truth is that the original form of ragtime was created by black musicians who used European musical forms. Ragtime was also influenced by blacks who danced the cotillion, a lively but formal eighteenth-century French dance. The cotillion had varied intricate patterns and steps similar to a march. The European-based march form of music was an important part of ragtime. Ragtime music, often mentioned as having early jazzlike traits, is both beautiful and complex. As black America's first non-folk music, ragtime was basically made up of piano compositions that were supposed to be played exactly as written. Some black musicians felt that ragtime limited their freedom of musical expression.

Scott Joplin has been called the Father of Ragtime Music. Although Joplin was formally trained in the European style, ragtime was his favorite kind of music. In 1899 he wrote the famous "Maple Leaf Rag." It is the first song to sell a million copies in the history of popular music.

Joplin was way ahead of his time. Many people in his day did not consider ragtime to be equal with what they felt was the "better music" of the white composers. He became discouraged that his music was not given proper recognition. Joplin made a statement that reflected his future hope for ragtime music: "Maybe fifty years after I am dead it will be [accepted]." Joplin died in New York in 1917, depressed and broke after trying to produce a ragtime opera called *Treemonisha*.

Almost fifty-three years after Joplin's death, his music underwent a tremendous revival. New recordings of his music were issued in 1970. In 1972 all of his known piano compositions were collected and published. In 1973 his music was used as the soundtrack of a popular movie starring Paul Newman called *The Sting*. In 1975 his ragtime folk opera *Treemonisha* was

Scott Joplin's opera Treemonisha *was revived and performed to rave reviews in 1975.*

performed in Houston, Texas, to rave reviews. *Treemonisha* also played on Broadway. Although Joplin did not live to see it, his ragtime music finally got the recognition that it deserved.

Most of the popular musicians of Joplin's time were traveling piano players who moved across the South and Midwest, performing in bars, roadhouses, or wherever they could. Most of them lived in the Mississippi Valley in the larger towns along the river. They were influenced by the folk songs and religious music of the people they lived among. They also brought their own original musical styles. This mixture of different musical forms made up this special way of playing the piano.

The cakewalk was a dance that the slaves did to make fun of the ways of white society. It became an important part of minstrelsy and was also popular during the time that ragtime was being developed. Several compositions were written for this dance, which came to be called rags.

Many early rags were called marches, such as Scott Joplin's "Combination March." March bands were very popular in the Midwest, where ragtime was developed. Although the formal structure of piano rags was more European than African, ragtime did have some strong connections with black American music. The rhythm in ragtime is African based.

A special style of ragtime music came from an area of New York called Tin Pan Alley. It got this name because the music played there had a "tinny-like" sound. Some famous piano players that performed in New York in the ragtime tradition, were Willie "The Lion" Smith, James P. Johnson, and Fats Waller. New York became the center of the music publishing world, and the exciting ragtime beat was a perfect match for the frantic and bustling mood of the city.

The music of Tin Pan Alley was mainly written by white composers who learned it from black musicians. This was very similar to what white minstrels had done with the music they heard around the slave quarters. Though the ragtime of Tin Pan Alley was popular, it was considered to be only a little more refined than the black ragtime.

Most black musicians felt that ragtime was not very original. The most exciting music was coming from Mississippi River towns such as Memphis and Saint Louis. A new style of music was being played in these places. It was based on ragtime but was called jazz.

FOUR

Africa, America, and Jazz

The influence of West African rhythms, European harmony, Latin American styles, and even West Indian forms have all contributed to the music of jazz. Jazz is mostly an instrumental music, although it has influenced a number of singers who perform in a jazz style. Ella Fitzgerald, Billie Holiday, and Sarah Vaughn were exciting jazz vocalists during this time.

Jazz music took many of its elements from ragtime and the blues. The combination of melody and emphasized rhythms of ragtime with added harmony and special orchestration has produced jazz. Jazz developed alongside the blues. Blues great W. C. Handy felt that jazz was another step in the development of black music. According to Handy, first there were the spirituals, then ragtime and the blues, and finally jazz. Jazz sprang up in the same area that the blues and ragtime did, which was in the major Southern towns along the Mississippi.

Ragtime was embraced by white America in its original form, but it was eventually changed by blacks to an early form of jazz. This change took place mainly due to the pioneering efforts of pianist Jelly Roll Morton.

Ferdinand Joseph "Jelly Roll" Morton was one of the first musicians to break out of the restricting way of playing piano rags, but his music was still rooted in ragtime. Morton's changes to ragtime made him one of the bridges to the ever developing music of piano jazz. As mentioned earlier, different aspects of jazz were also being developed by other musicians during the early 1900s. Morton is considered an early jazz pianist with a link to ragtime. His fresh and innovative approach to playing ragtime became one of the elements of jazz.

One of the special traits of jazz is its tendency to encourage improvisation from the musician who is performing it. This means that a jazz musician can make up and play different notes that may not be on the sheet music. This is one reason that jazz sounds fresh and original. The African-American tradition of musicians making up parts of songs as they are performing them also reminds us of the black fieldworkers and the singers of spirituals. Jazz also borrows elements of the swinging part of ragtime music. Jazz often becomes a test of a musician's technical skills, imagination, and artistry.

A brilliant young black bandleader named James Reese Europe was aware of the importance of blacks developing their own music based on their African traditions. He once commented, "We must strike out for ourselves, we must develop our own ideas, and conceive an orchestration adapted to our own abilities and instincts. . . ."

Europe and his band played for New York society, including the wealthy Astors and Vanderbilts. His band played also at Carnegie Hall in 1914 and went to France to play for the troops during World War I. When Europe returned to New York, he said, "I have come back from France more firmly convinced than ever that Negroes should write Negro music. We have our own racial feeling and if we try to copy whites we will make bad copies . . . if we are to develop in America we must develop along our own lines. . . ." Unfortunately he was not able to develop these ideas further. He was killed by one of his own band members on May 9, 1919.

Lt. Jim Europe was director of the 365th U.S. Infantry band, known as the "Hellfighters Band."

The world's first exposure to jazz was probably around 1917 when the Original Dixieland Jazz Band released its first recordings. New Orleans jazz is sometimes called Dixieland jazz. It originated from military marches, black southern blues music, and the influence of French and Creole culture. During and after the First World War, many musicians traveled up the Mississippi to find places where they could make a living with their music. Jazz was presented to a broader audience when musicians like King Oliver and Louis Armstrong left New Orleans for Chicago.

Daniel Louis Armstrong, who became known as Satchmo (short for "satchel mouth"), was born in New Orleans in 1900. Armstrong was an African-American jazz trumpeter, singer, and bandleader, and was one of the most popular musicians of his day. As an improvisational genius, he had a great influence on the melodic development of jazz. Armstrong was one of the main people responsible for the rise of the solo jazz artist. White jazz artists like Bix Beiderbecke, who began playing piano but became famous playing the cornet, were greatly influenced by Oliver and Armstrong.

New Orleans is considered an important city in the development of jazz, but there were similar styles of jazz music that came out of Memphis, Saint Louis, Dallas, Kansas City, and other towns. Northern towns like Chicago also introduced some of the earliest forms of jazz. Chicagoans claim that jazz was invented there by a man called Jasbo Brown. Brown played trombone and performed W. C. Handy's "Memphis Blues" and other songs with a wild, creative style. He was said to be able to make his instrument "talk" by putting his derby hat over the end of his trombone. Legend has it that Brown played such exciting music that the patrons of the nightclub would yell, "More, Jas, more." Some people claim that this is how the music came to be known as jazz.

From the 1920s to the 1940s swing music was popular. The small New Orleans jazz bands continued to play, but the swing movement called for larger groups that featured soloists with prearranged musical backgrounds. The orchestras of Duke Ellington, Count Basie, and Benny Goodman were especially successful during this period.

King Oliver's Creole Jazz Band was well known in the 1920s.
A young Louis Armstrong is shown playing trumpet.

The ideas that Duke Ellington brought to the full orchestra began in the late 1920s. Although Ellington had taken piano lessons at an early age, he was mainly a self-taught musician. He believed that improvisation was important and that anyone who depended too much on written music would have limited self-expression. Many of Ellington's early works were unwritten musical arrangements. As he began to compose more on paper, his music often reflected suggestions from orchestra members. Sometimes he borrowed ideas from their improvised solos. His unique style came from exploring new musical forms that added sweet harmonizing melodies to exciting dissonant chords. His brilliant songwriting included a broad range of styles, from breathtakingly romantic ballads to hard-driving swing music.

In late 1927 Ellington became the house bandleader of the famous Cotton Club in Harlem. Although the performers were black, the club's entertainment was designed to appeal to its mostly white customers. The floor shows featured bizarre African scenes that, although full of racial stereotypes, were the setting for what would be called Ellington's "jungle music."

Musicians were sought who had developed their own distinctive styles of playing, then Ellington would write compositions to showcase their musical skills. The Ellington Orchestra attracted and kept talented musicians for extended periods. During the early 1940s these included violinist Ray Nance, trumpeter Rex Stewart, trombonist Tricky Sam Nanton, clarinetist Harry Carney, saxophonist Johnny Hodges, and percussionist Sonny Greer.

Ellington composed or arranged over 1,000 pieces of music between 1920 and 1970, which was an unprecedented achievement. Notable works include "Black and Tan Fantasy," "Caravan," "Perdido," "Do Nothin' Til You Hear From Me," "Black, Brown and Beige," "Mood Indigo," and "Satin Doll." Ellington's talented arranger Billy Strayhorn wrote the classic "Take the A Train" and "Lush Life" for the Ellington orchestra in

1939. In later years Ellington wrote for television a history of jazz called *A Drum Is a Woman* and a show celebrating the centennial of the Emancipation Proclamation called *My People*.

Every big-band leader and composer who came after Ellington, along with musicians from other areas of American music, was influenced by his compositional style. In addition to many other prizes and honors, Ellington was awarded the Medal of Freedom, the nation's highest civilian honor. In 1974, shortly after his orchestra made tours of Europe, Africa, and the United States, Ellington died of cancer.

Count Basie and his orchestra offered a fresh approach to the elaborate arrangements of other swing-era big bands. From 1937 to 1943 Basie popularized a simple bluesy method that was known as the Kansas City jazz style. The foundation of the Basie sound was a smooth, steady, and relaxed rhythm, which was ably provided by bassist Walter Paige, drummer Jo Jones, and guitarist Freddie Green. These musicians were the perfect complement to Basie's unique piano style.

Unlike Basie or Ellington, who were African American, Benny Goodman was the son of Jewish immigrants from Russia. He played the clarinet in a boldly swinging style that appealed to mass audiences. He was especially noted for his creative arrangements for big bands and the development of a highly improvisational combo. Goodman was the first major bandleader to bring together black and white musicians, at a time when most groups were racially segregated. Goodman's combo was also the first interracial jazz group to perform in public. It included Teddy Wilson, Lionel Hampton, and drummer Gene Krupa. Goodman soon grew to become one of the most popular big-band leaders of the 1930s.

In the 1940s the "cool jazz" music of bebop, often just called bop, became a musical protest against the smooth and danceable styles of swing. It was a new and different kind of jazz that used complex rhythms and harmonies rather than the traditional songlike melodies played by swing orchestras. Alto saxophonist Charlie "Bird" Parker and trumpeter Dizzy

Gillespie became leaders in this new style. Jazz pianist Thelonious Monk also became a major jazz innovator in bop style.

Jazz continued to become more progressive throughout the 1950s by using the harmonies of bop, but with less complex rhythms and melodies. This style was made popular in California by tenor sax player Lester Young. Pianist Dave Brubeck and tenor sax player Stan Getz were also important figures in the West Coast jazz movement.

Jazz pianist Thelonious Monk

From the mid-1950s to the late 1960s another jazz movement took place that was called hard bop. This music further refined bop while introducing harmonies and melodies taken from gospel and blues influences.

Hard bop was showcased by musicians such as tenor saxophonists John Coltrane and Sonny Rollins. Many modern jazz musicians such as trumpeter Miles Davis have fused other types of music—for example, rock 'n' roll—with jazz.

Jazz is an African-American musical tradition, but it is not a music that is altogether by or for black people. Some of the white jazz musicians that we have mentioned could be considered innovators because some of them influenced important black musicians. Frankie Trumbauer influenced Coleman Hawkins, and Harlem saxophone styles of playing were similar to the style of the Guy Lombardo Orchestra's saxophone section.

In 1948 jazz drummer Art Blakey visited Africa. He produced an album called *The African Beat* with the Afro Drum Ensemble using drummers from Nigeria, Senegal, Jamaica, and the United States. Jazzy saxophone solos combined with West African drum rhythms gave this album a different sound from the other jazz records of that time. Traditional native African songs influenced much of Blakey's music from that time on.

In May 1956 Louis Armstrong visited the Gold Coast in Africa. He was convinced that his ancestors came from that region. He went as a goodwill ambassador from the United States. Drummers there pounded out a traditional African song that they renamed "All For You Louie!" Armstrong and his band invited the drummers and other African musicians to join them as they played for the crowd of over 100,000 West African jazz fans.

The sound of jazz is rooted in the call-and-response style that can be

Drummer Art Blakey led the Jazz Messengers combo from the 1950s until he died in 1990. Many great jazz soloists trained with this group.

traced back to African musical traditions. The field hollers and shouts used by black preachers and their church members were also an important element of jazz.

The music by Miles Davis on his recording of "So What" is a good example of instrumentation reflecting these same African traits. His use of high-pitched tones is meant to sound like the human voice, and strong feelings can be heard in the squeaks and squawks of the jazz saxophone. Moanlike crying and yelling sounds that reflect the hardships of slavery can be heard in the growl of the trumpet. Johnny Green's arrangement of "Body & Soul" as played by tenor saxophonist Coleman Hawkins is another example of this expression of emotion.

Jazz has gone in different directions and through many changes. A number of the current traditional jazz artists are attempting to give jazz a more mainstream appeal by working with some of the popular rap music groups. Jazzrapping groups like Digable Planets "sample" music from jazzmen such as Sonny Rollins and Art Blakey. (Sampling is when a rap artist uses an excerpt from another musician's recording.) Rapper Guru's recording entitled *Jazzmatazz Volume: 1* combines jazz and rap. Guru said, "I want to make older people appreciate hip-hop and get my homeboys to appreciate jazz."

Jazz has been influenced by and has influenced many American musical styles. A major change that has occurred in jazz over the last fifty years has been a lessened emphasis on jazz as a music for people to dance to. In jazz's earlier form it was probably closest to its African roots. It seems that today jazz is closer to being a more classical music.

Trumpeter Wynton Marsalis electrified the traditional classical music and jazz scenes with his debut in the 1980s. Marsalis's style is loosely based on the work of Miles Davis and is combined with classical and jazz techniques as well as elements uniquely his own. His 1983 album, *Think of One* took the musical world by storm.

Born in 1961 to a musical family in New Orleans, Marsalis was introduced to jazz by his father, Ellis, a professional pianist. Marsalis played in marching bands, jazz groups, and professional orchestras before receiving an invitation to tour and record with Art Blakey's Jazz Messengers and Herbie Hancock. In 1982 Marsalis won Musician of the Year from the readers of *Downbeat* magazine, and in 1984 he received Grammy Awards in both the classical music and jazz categories.

Wynton Marsalis plays both classical and jazz music. Here he plays a tribute to popular jazzman Dizzy Gillespie, who died in 1993.

Marsalis has managed to bridge the gap between European classical music and classical jazz. He is the first and only performer to be internationally recognized as one of the best musicians in both styles. He has said that he believes that jazz is more sophisticated and technically challenging than European classical music. Marsalis says, "I love being a jazz musician. . . . My whole life I wanted to be a jazzman . . . because it just seems like jazz music is the real soul of the Afro-American."

Jazz can easily be considered the classical music of African Americans. It is music that has its roots in African culture but that has grown into a truly unique art form.

FIVE

THE GOSPEL SOUND

Gospel music in America dates back to the 1920s, but it first became popular during the years of the Great Depression. In storefront churches the sounds of a jumping piano, hand clapping, shaking tambourines, and harmonious voices singing of the love of Jesus gave hope to black people as they tried to cope with desperate poverty. Elements of the early black spirituals with roots going back to Africa can be heard in gospel music. The South African a cappella group Ladysmith Black Mambazo sings in a style that is reminiscent of early black spirituals.

Since gospel music was the creation of songwriters, it is different from the spirituals. No one knows who wrote many of the spirituals, which are considered part of the folk music tradition of blacks during slavery. Gospel music was written by popular songwriters of the day.

It was not until the 1930s that modern black gospel music began to become popular. Professor Thomas A. Dorsey was called the Father of Gospel Music. From 1939 to 1941 Dorsey took his own compositions and singers with him as he traveled from church to church. Mahalia Jackson became popular traveling with Dorsey and performing his original songs. Partly due to Dorsey's efforts, Jackson and many other gospel singers received much recognition of their singing talents.

Dorsey began his early musical career as a jazz pianist who accompanied blues singer Ma Rainey. Dorsey also played with the great Bessie Smith. Under the name Georgia Tom he composed music and also recorded blues with Ma Rainey. It was shortly after Dorsey's success as a blues musician that he turned to religious music. He was first attracted to gospel music in 1921 when he recorded a song in the Pentecostal hymnal, "Gospel Pearls," although he continued to play and record the blues. In 1932 he recorded his most famous song, "Precious Lord," which became a gospel classic. This was the year that he turned to producing gospel music exclusively. Mahalia Jackson called Dorsey "our Irving Berlin."

Mahalia Jackson was born in New Orleans and first sang in her father's church. When she died in 1972, she was the best-known gospel singer in the world.

The influence of popular music, blues, and even jazz was seen in early black gospel songs. Gospel music has in turn influenced many modern music forms, including soul, rhythm and blues, and rock. Early gospel music was usually performed by a choir accompanied by a piano. Later developments included the addition of electric guitars, saxophones, drums, basses, and trumpets to the performance.

Much of the gospel music that has come from African Americans has its roots in Pentecostal or Holiness churches. It is interesting how the Pentecostal style of singing and playing music would eventually affect religious as well as popular music.

Holiness churches accepted and encouraged the use of percussion instruments such as the tambourine, the triangle, and the drums. This is a direct influence of African musical traditions. In country churches the guitar was used. Guitars were then replaced in the city by the piano. Other instruments that were more often associated with jazz, such as trumpets, trombones, and saxophones, were added to express the excitement of an especially moving service.

The role of the black preacher was essentially tied to the development of black gospel music. His ability to get an immediate and vocal response to his sermon from the congregation established the mood of the service. His message would often merge into song, which became the basis for many styles of popular music.

Black gospel is often said to have the sound and feeling of the early forms of jazz. Just as jazz and the blues grew and developed into distinctively different forms, so did black gospel music. Jazz has also been influenced by gospel music from the Holiness churches. A classic example of a gospel-jazz song that links these ideas together is "When the Saints Go Marching In."

From the 1930s to the 1950s black female singers dominated modern gospel music, just as they had done with the classic blues of the 1920s. Early blues singers Ma Rainey and Bessie Smith had much influence on the singing styles of the first group of popular gospel singers. Gospel great Mahalia Jackson once said of Bessie Smith, "Bessie was my favorite but I never let people know I listened to her. Mamie Smith, the other famous blues singer, had a pretty voice, but Bessie's had more soul in it. She dug right down and kept it in you. Her music haunted you even when she stopped singing."

A second wave of gospel singers brought forth several styles that had much in common with jazz singing. The technique of sliding into different pitches, the use of repetitive phrases, and bending notes and rhythms were used by Clara Ward, Marion Williams, Ruth Davis, and Albertina Walker. The refrain from the popular gospel song "How I Got Over" by Clara Ward is given below:

LEAD: *How I got over*

CHORUS: *How I got over*

LEAD: *How I got over*

CHORUS: *How I got over*

LEAD AND CHORUS: *My soul looks back and wonders*
How I got over

The piano accompaniment for gospel music was greatly influenced by ragtime and other popular styles. It was not long before bass and drums were also added. The format was basically a lead (usually female) singer with both male and female voices providing background vocals.

Another type of group that was important in the history of black gospel was the all-male quartet. Early groups from the 1920s and 1930s would sing with no instrumental accompaniment. They were influenced by the style of the early spirituals as sung by groups like the Fisk Jubilee Singers. From the 1930s to the mid-1940s male singing groups began to take on more jazz traits. Several groups became popular during this period, including the Soul Stirrers, the Blue Jay Singers, the Dixie Hummingbirds, and the Golden Gate Quartet.

From the 1950s to the 1970s modern gospel music has taken two main directions, either contemporary or traditional. The difference has more to do with how the public perceives the music rather than its actual style. Traditional gospel is usually performed within the framework of a church service as a part of an overall religious experience. On the other hand, contemporary gospel is a source of entertainment, although the effect of being soothed and comforted as in a religious service may still be achieved. This is not to say that all traditional gospel music is confined to churches, but the participation of the audience gives it the same kind of church atmosphere.

The Reverend James Cleveland became one of the most important figures in contemporary gospel music. Cleveland sang with Professor Thomas Dorsey and Roberta Martin when he was a boy. He was Mahalia Jackson's paperboy and he often listened to her sing. Cleveland began singing at the Pilgrim Baptist Church, where Thomas Dorsey was the choir director. He later became a famous gospel singer but used his voice so much that he strained it. Cleveland said, "That's why it sounds like a foghorn. Lots of

The Reverend James Cleveland speaking at the nineteenth annual convention of the Gospel Music Workshop of America in 1986

folks call me the Louis Armstrong of Gospel." He shared similar singing styles with Shirley Caesar, Dorothy Love Coates, and the Barrett Sisters. The Gospel Music Workshop of America was formed by Cleveland in 1968 to help improve the gospel choirs of African-American churches.

Andrae Crouch shaped much of contemporary gospel music. His music is arranged in a style that sounds closer to popular music. This may explain why his music appeals to a broader audience. Groups, too, such as the Edwin Hawkins Singers, have made successful crossovers to appeal to the general public. Their song "Oh Happy Day" became a number-one hit on the popular music charts in the mid-1970s. In that same tradition the gospel singing of the Winans family, especially BeBe and CeCe Winans, has succeeded in attracting a broad audience.

Gospel music strongly influenced Ray Charles, who based several songs on original gospel tunes. The gospel sound is also evident in rhythm and blues and soul music as reflected by singers Little Richard, Aretha Franklin, and Al Green. Franklin recorded a gospel album, *Amazing Grace*, which sold over a million copies. Black gospel has also influenced the music of Otis Redding, James Brown, and B. B. King.

In the spirit of the music that the Fisk Jubilee Singers made popular, a unique a cappella singing group called Sweet Honey in the Rock was formed in 1973 by Bernice Johnson Reagon. Since it began, Sweet Honey in the Rock has sung songs about spiritual and political liberation, love, and social responsibility. The only instrument that accompanies the group is an African *shekere*, which is a kind of rattle made from a gourd surrounded by dried peas or beads.

The group has sung in many different musical styles including gospel, folk, blues, and rap. Reagon understands that their music was built on the legacy inherited from groups like the Fisk Jubilee Singers. She says, "There ought to be some constant way you can say thank you to acknowledge that you stand on the ground that was laid by other people who came before you."

RHYTHM AND BLUES

Rhythm and blues, now usually shortened to R&B, refers to a number of closely related black musical styles that became popular after the Second World War. R&B was similar to earlier forms of black American music in that it was based on a mixture of European influences, syncopated jazz rhythms, tonal inflections, and the flatted blues chords. The R&B style grew out of the country blues of the South. The elements of hollers, work chants, and gospel music from black churches were incorporated into R&B to express many deeply felt emotions.

The earliest form of R&B was heard in the dance music of the big bands of the 1930s and 1940s. This music was played in the style of the jump band. Jump bands were known for their emphasis on strong rhythm, exciting saxophone solos, and shouted blues vocals. Most of the larger jump bands had vanished by the early 1950s.

A second form of R&B began in the bars and nightclubs of the South Side of Chicago in the 1940s, where it was often called Chicago blues. Performers such as Muddy Waters, Sonny Boy Williamson, and Howlin' Wolf usually played very loudly. The instruments used to accompany these singers were electric guitar, harmonica, electric bass, electric piano or organ, and drums. A number of the songs' lyrics and vocals borrowed extensively from the rural blues. The music had a strong beat and was made for dancing.

Still another major form of R&B was mainly vocal. Instrumental accompaniment could vary from full orchestra to none at all. This form was usually performed by a group whose singing utilized close harmonies and a medium-to-slow tempo. Black gospel church musical influences were obvious. The lead singer performed the high-pitched notes and often either sang on top of the wordless chords of the others or led them in a call-and-response pattern.

In 1949 this style became identified as a new sound in black music. The term *rhythm and blues* was created by record companies and trade publications like *Billboard* in the 1950s. Rhythm and blues (R&B) was used to label music by blacks that was specifically marketed to a black audience. White-owned companies had previously used terms such as *ebony*, *sepia*, and *race music* to describe and segregate this music from mainstream popular music. R&B reflected the beginnings of a breakdown of the earlier separation of black and white music markets. However during the 1950s and 1960s R&B was also called rock 'n' roll by the music industry to hide its black origins and make it more appealing to white audiences.

Bandleader Louis Jordan was a popular musician. His group was called the Tympany Five and played music that was known as rhythm and blues. For their own enjoyment the group played a bouncy, shuffling boogie rhythm that made it impossible to sit still. They were the early pioneers of a style that would earn Jordan the title Father of Rhythm and Blues.

The early records of the Tympany Five included "Pinetop Boogie" and "Caldonia Boogie." Woody Herman, a popular white bandleader, had a best-selling record that was based on Jordan's "Caldonia Boogie." But the most successful record that Jordan ever had was "Choo Ch'Boogie," which

Louis Jordan (in hat) and his band in the 1940s. He later became a big star of Aladdin Records.

sold over 1 million copies by 1946. Jordan's music appealed to the mainstream white audience, although the subjects of the songs, the way they were performed, and the performers were all black. Louis Jordan once said of his band, before his death in 1975, "I did everything with a big band. I made the blues jump." What Jordan was referring to was a smaller version of the traditional big band that was so popular in the late forties and early fifties.

Jordan had a great influence on other black musicians, such as Johnny Otis and Chuck Berry. Berry would go on to became a major player in the development of styles of music identified with teenage rock 'n' roll. Bo Diddley was also a performer of early R&B.

R&B has elements of gospel, big-band swing, and blues. It changed from the typical blues group when the electric guitar was added to play the lead part, along with an electric bass. A powerful drummer, a piano, at least one saxophone, and a small male or female vocal group were also used so that the blues singer could get a response to his or her calls and key phrases. It was from the roots of R&B that the music of disco, soul, funk, and rap would spring forth.

The singing style of R&B can vary from the moaning cry of Delta bluesmen to the smooth vibrato and jazzy inflection of city blues singers. R&B singers attempt to bring the swelling excitement of gospel music to their performances. In following this style, the words of a song are sometimes shouted as well as sung. Joe Turner used this technique when he recorded "Chains of Love" in Kansas City in 1950. Turner's classic R&B hit in 1954 was "Shake, Rattle and Roll."

Unfortunately many R&B performers were disappointed that they were not given what they felt was suitable recognition by the white-dominated record industry. This was compounded by the fact that in the 1950s racial segregation was still in place. Blacks were not allowed to go to Broadway theaters, movie houses, or nightclubs. It took the civil rights movement of the 1960s to stir up a sense of pride and dignity in African Americans, which would soon be reflected in R&B music.

Many record companies were biased against black singers because they felt the black singers' musical styles were rough and would appeal only to black audiences. In its attempts to appeal to a broader audience (therefore increasing record sales) the music industry began the practice of the "cover." This involved taking black hit songs and rearranging and rereleasing them for white artists to perform. When this happened, the original black version of the song would be dominated by the white cover version.

For example, one of the major female R&B singers was Willie Mae "Big Mama" Thornton. It was Thornton who first sang "(You're Nothin' but a) Hound Dog." Most listeners were unaware that Thornton's "Hound

Dog" had been the number-three hit of 1953 when Elvis Presley did a different version of it three years later, making it a gigantic hit.

Thornton never received the recognition that her talent warranted, but she became a great influence on the soulful sounds of Aretha Franklin and Janis Joplin. Joplin, a white female blues singer, idolized and imitated Thornton. Joplin recorded a powerful rendition of Thornton's song "Ball and Chain."

Two of the premier artists of R&B were Fats Domino and B. B. King, who both made successful recordings in the early 1950s. Domino was different from King with his New Orleans jazz and boogie piano style. King was the undisputed master of the electric guitar, in the tradition of T-Bone Walker. Domino produced a number-one R&B hit called "Goin' Home." It was followed by the R&B classics "Ain't It a Shame," "Blueberry Hill," and "I'm Walkin'." His records became crossover hits and continued to be best-sellers, going gold up until the 1960s.

The rough blues style of B. B. King seemed to limit his appeal to the record-buying public. This resulted in a smaller number of best-selling recordings. King scored a number-one hit with "Three O' Clock Blues" and again with "You Know I Love You." He garnered number two on the R&B charts for four more songs. In 1970 one of the

Willie Mae "Big Mama" Thornton influenced singers Aretha Franklin and Janis Joplin.

In 1994 B. B. King received a Grammy Award for Best Traditional Blues Album. The album was Blues Summit.

most popular King recordings, "The Thrill Is Gone," went to number three on the R&B list.

King gathered a loyal following of both black and white fans by traveling the country for over thirty years giving over 300 performances a year. His efforts brought him three prestigious awards in 1982—a Grammy for his album *There Must Be a Better World Somewhere*, a W. C. Handy Award for Blues Entertainer of the Year, and a special Commendation for Excellence from BMI music company for his creative talents in the field of R&B.

SEVEN

THE SOUL SOUND

Soul music represents some of the most exciting elements of black music in American culture. The term *soul* describes a music that has been influenced by a number of black musical styles. Soul is a product of the swinging instrumental rhythms of R&B blended with the strongly voiced vocal style of gospel.

The development of soul can be compared to the important role that music played in traditional African culture and society. African music, like soul, was often played for enjoyment. But African music was also an important part of the way that people connected to one another and to their society through commonly shared ideals and experiences in daily life. In a similar way soul provided a musical connection between black people and their common experiences in America. Soul was more than just music. It was also an attitude that black people should not sacrifice the African part of their African-American identity to be accepted into white mainstream society.

Having soul meant that one looked at life in America from a black perspective. Anything could have soul if it had roots in the black experience in America. This unique view of American culture and society gave rise to popular terms like *soul food*, *soul sister*, and *soul man*. People could only begin to understand soul if they understood the effect that hundreds of years of racism had on both blacks and whites.

In 1968 James Brown electrified millions of young African Americans with his hard-rapping vocal anthem of black pride, "Say It Loud (I'm Black and I'm Proud)!" Brown's use of call-and-response techniques combined with a machine-gun delivery defined the era of soul while laying the early foundations of rap music.

Soul came out during a time when many African Americans were rediscovering their proud African cultural tradition. From the late 1950s to the early 1960s black R&B had been mixed with white country and western music, transforming it into white-oriented rock 'n' roll. Soul, like earlier black musical styles, was formed by a people who were segregated from mainstream white society. What made soul different from other musical styles was that it was not successfully borrowed by whites, as blues and jazz had been.

Charles Keil, who wrote *Urban Blues*, once explained that every time black styles of music are taken and sold to white America, it "forces a return, by blacks, to the well of their tradition to draw forth fresh material that will remain off limits to whites, at least for a while." Soul was a kind of musical protest against white America's exploitation of black musical styles. It was often difficult for any musician to play soul from the written music alone. This was music that a performer had to feel as well as hear. Soul musicians often spoke in a way that communicated unwritten musical concepts. This influence came from African-based oral traditions.

African Americans were aware of their second-class status in American culture and society. Many realized that few black musicians had become financially successful and most were still poor. The civil rights and black nationalist movements of the 1950s through the 1970s brought out many ideas about ending economic oppression, racial segregation, and discrimination against African Americans. Soul music often spoke to issues regarding the struggles of black people in America. At times soul was like the early black spirituals that gave directions to runaway slaves while also providing inspiration and hope.

Someone once said that at any point in history the condition of African Americans is reflected by their music at that time. Sometimes soul music contributed marching themes for the civil rights movement as both blacks and whites boldly demanded equal opportunity for all Americans and an end to racism.

Soul often uses the call-and-response techniques that are common traits of traditional African music. It also has the squeals and moans of rhythm and blues. Soul musicians such as James Brown, Wilson Pickett, Lou Rawls, Otis Redding, and Aretha Franklin could speak directly to their audiences by singing this way.

The majority of soul musicians began singing in black churches. B. B. King once said, "In James [Brown]'s and Aretha [Franklin]'s case they are more like in church, a [black] Holiness church, where everybody's getting the beat, getting the feeling." What King observed is that soul singers, similar to gospel singers, demand the emotional involvement and participation of the audience. Black disc jockey Bill Williams, from Detroit radio station WCHB, commented during the 1960s that "soul music derives from the gospel thing and the camp meeting thing, the plantation scenes and all the old blues singers who started singing songs of sorrow. Most of these songs had the same feel, the same basic pattern, and the soul music we play today is an outgrowth of these things."

In the song "Talkin' 'Bout Soul" Marvin L. Simms touches on the "feeling" of soul:

> *Everybody talkin' 'bout soul,*
> *How it make you feel now,*

But I just want to know baby,
Do they really know the deal now
All you got to do is feel it,
I'm talkin' 'bout soul . . .

Popular rock 'n' roll tunes were sometimes totally transformed into a soul style. When Ray Charles recorded the popular Beatles song "Eleanor Rigby," it was changed into a soul hit. Other Beatles classics changed to a soulful style were "Ticket to Ride," by Willie Walker, and "Day Tripper," by the Vontastics. Aretha Franklin's soulful rendition of Paul Simon and Art Garfunkel's megahit rock song "Bridge Over Troubled Water" took that song to new musical heights.

Ray Charles is a popular singer with a style influenced by gospel, rhythm and blues, and jazz.

Historians of American popular music generally agree that soul music began in the mid-1950s with Ray Charles. Ray Charles was born in 1930 in Albany, Georgia. Blind since the age of six, he learned to play several instruments, including the clarinet, alto sax, trumpet, organ, and piano. Charles preferred playing the piano and was influenced by the great pianist-singer Nat King Cole. Soon he developed his own special style. His performances contained a mixture of gospel shouts and blues.

Charles began his musical career by singing the blues in a style similar to that of Charles

Brown, a popular blues singer of that time. What set Ray Charles apart from other musicians was the way he took popular gospel songs and redid them in a nonreligious way. In 1954 he changed the gospel standard "My Jesus Is All the World to Me" to "I've Got a Woman." The next year he gave a similar treatment to "This Little Light of Mine," an old gospel classic by Clara Ward. He changed some of the words to reflect his feelings about his girlfriend, and the title became "This Little Girl of Mine." Many older people considered the merging of sacred and "worldly" music to be sacrilegious or in bad taste. Blues musician Big Bill Broonzy was opposed to Ray Charles's style of music and said, "Ray is mixin' the blues with spirituals. That's wrong. . . . He should be singin' in the church."

As Charles's music became more popular, he broke down the traditional separation between blues and gospel music. This is important because it marks a return to another major factor of African cultural and musical tradition. In Africa musical expression was not separated from everyday life. Charles was going back to his African roots.

In the 1960s R&B began to make way for soul music. Ray Charles, more than anyone else, successfully brought the blues sound together with gospel music.

Motown and Stax were two black-owned music companies that were instrumental in taking soul music to a broader audience that included whites. These companies discovered, promoted, produced the music for, and marketed most of the soul music artists of the 1960s and 1970s.

The companies represented two separate but related movements in soul music: the Detroit sound, which is probably better known as the Motown sound, and the "down-home" Memphis sound promoted by Stax. Music historian Arnold Shaw described the difference between the two this way: "If Motown is the northern ghetto expanding into the white world of sleek automobiles and plush clubs . . . then Stax is the Mississippi River overflowing the banks of the 1960s. Inescapably, the Memphis Sound had more grit, gravel and mud in it than the Detroit Sound."

The Motown sound started in Detroit, Michigan. It was a reflection of a new class of enterprising and upwardly mobile young African Americans who wanted to use their music to become successful members of mainstream urban society. Black soul singers, musicians, and record companies realized that in order to compete with their larger and mostly white counterparts, they had to change their music to a style that would appeal to whites. No one understood the need for soul music to cross over better than a young black autoworker and former boxer from Detroit, Michigan, named Berry Gordy, Jr. Gordy was the founder of Motown Records.

Motown had a reputation for using stringed instruments in its music. Players were sometimes selected from the Detroit Symphony Orchestra. Gordy believed that all of Motown's performers had to have the highest qualities of musical skill and showmanship. He would carefully choose the musical selections and arrangements and make sure that every song and dance step was delivered perfectly. Gordy was so particular about the image he was trying to create that he even established a finishing school for his black artists so that they would know proper etiquette. Gordy's remarkable ability to market his music and performers in a way that appealed to both whites and blacks resulted in his capture of the mainstream musical market.

Soon records with the Motown sound, a mixture of soulful ballads, finger-popping rhythms, and smooth harmonies, made the Supremes, the Temptations, Marvin Gaye, and Stevie Wonder internationally famous. Motown became known for producing romantic music that had a steady, driving beat. Michael Jackson and the Jackson Five began their careers recording with Motown.

Stax was begun in 1959 by Jim Stewart and his sister, Estelle Axton. The name of the company came from the first two letters of their last names. Stax developed its soul sounds as much through its studio musicians as though its vocal stars. The studio band was known as the M.G.'s (short for Memphis Group). The group included two blacks, organist/pianist Booker T. Jones and drummer Al Jackson, and two whites, lead guitarist Steve Cropper and bass player Donald "Duck" Dunn. The group brought together musical experiences from the blues heritage as well as white country and black gospel music. The integration of these different styles was what made the Memphis sound unique.

Jones said that the Memphis sound "started in the Negro church in the South. The music was really soul-searching. It was enough to make the listener cry at times. We've retained the basic elements of this church music in the Memphis Sound." The Memphis sound was a mixture of popular white American song forms, African-American vocals, a behind-the-beat rhythm, country and western bass lines, and gospel sounds coming from the horns, voices, and piano.

The Stax studio band began performing in the late 1960s as Booker T. and the M.G.'s. Stax and its related company Volt produced their first major recording, entitled "Green Onions," an instrumental that was number one on *Billboard* magazine's R&B list. The song soon crossed over to the Top Ten Of Pop charts, where it became a gold record in 1967. That same year the group became the Top Instrumental Combo (moving up over the popular white R&B group of Herb Alpert and the Tijuana Brass) in *Billboard* magazine's year-end poll.

R&B singer, dancer, and deejay Rufus Thomas was an early artist associated with Stax. He began in 1963 with the song-and-dance sensation "Walking the Dog," which was followed by several other dance hits. Carla Thomas, Rufus's daughter, began her solo career with Stax in 1961 with a song she wrote, "(Gee Whiz) Look at His Eyes." Carla went to Atlantic Records, then in 1966 came back to Stax, where she had another hit song, "B-A-B-Y." She received the title, Queen of Memphis Soul after an album she did with Otis Redding, *The King and the Queen*.

The most important singers in the Stax/Volt lineup were Otis Redding and Isaac Hayes. Hayes was an incredible songwriter and performer. He wrote several classic songs for the soul duo Sam and Dave. Hayes attained superstardom in the early 1970s with his *Hot Buttered Soul* album. Later

The Stax studio band was known as Booker T. and the M.G.'s. This group promoted the Memphis Sound of soul music.

came the soundtrack album for the movie *Shaft*, for which he received an Academy Award for best musical score.

Through the efforts of Gordy, Stewart, and others, soul music became one of the most popular styles of black music in America. Soul music began to overshadow the blues in the 1960s and then merged with R&B during the 1970s and 1980s to become a Southern-influenced style of black popular music. Many people who enjoyed soul music when they were young believe that it was the best music ever produced by African Americans.

EIGHT

THE ROAD TO ROCK 'N' ROLL

America is often called the human melting pot of the world. Rock 'n' roll music is also a melting pot. This country has brought together an uneasy mix of people of various colors and cultures. Like America, rock 'n' roll is also a tense mixture of different musical styles, cultural traditions, and rhythmic forms. Black American musical styles rooted in African rhythms and cultural traditions make up the foundation of rock 'n' roll.

The music has changed over the years from its original form. Today it is simply called rock. Rock has branched off to new musical directions and now covers such a broad area that it is not always easy to define. A look at the history of some important musical developments is necessary to better understand what rock is and how it was formed.

Rock 'n' roll came about as a result of the direct influence of African-American musical traditions. Like the blues, rock is music intended for a singer who is backed up by one or more electric guitars, a bass guitar, and often a piano or other keyboard instrument and drums. Rock is taken from a recent generation of black urban blues. The common practice of adding a saxophone and a backup vocal group is a direct influence of R&B. The development of creative new ways to play traditional instruments became an element of the blues that later became a defining characteristic of rock.

The earliest forms of rock came from a mixture of white country music and the old foot-stomping, loud, howling blues of the Mississippi Delta and parts of the Midwest. It had an easily identifiable beat that was especially suited for vigorous dancing. The sound was marked by heavily amplified guitars, offbeat rhythms (what the Beatles would later call backbeat), and suggestive lyrics. This music was called rockabilly: a combination of hillbilly (country) and rock and roll (blues and R&B).

In 1951 a white Cleveland record-store owner named Leo Mintz began to notice that white teenagers were buying black R&B records. These records could only be heard on the black radio stations, which meant that the music was appealing to an audience outside of the black neighborhoods. Young white people had begun to acquire a taste for black music.

In the same year, white radio station WCJ in Cleveland had just hired a new disk jockey (DJ) named Alan Freed. Freed found out about the popularity of black R&B among white teenagers and decided to begin playing black R&B records. He knew that white-oriented radio stations would not play black music, but he persuaded his boss to let him try a new program. Aware that he would have to be careful that he did not offend a large portion of his white audience, he cleverly disguised his new radio program by calling it "Moondog's Rock 'n' Roll Party."

The term *rock 'n' roll* was unknown at the time to most whites but had been commonly used for years by black singers as a slang word that sometimes meant dancing. The words were used in a number of black R&B songs beginning in the late 1940s, such as "Rock All Night" by the Ravens, "Good Rockin' Tonight" by Roy Brown, and "All She Wants to Do is Rock," by Wynonie Harris. Freed not only played black R&B records, but he also arranged live stage shows of black R&B performers for mostly white audiences. It was not long before white teenagers were calling R&B music rock 'n' roll.

White record companies began to record black popular music so that they could sell records to the black audience. The most popular records were advertised in several music trade publications. From 1920 to 1948 recordings by African-American performers for white-owned record companies were called "race records."

Racial prejudices and fears about the lyrics used on recordings caused most publications to hide the origins of hit black-produced records under titles like Folk and Blues, What's Hot in Harlem, or Sepia Hits. In 1948 Paul Ackerman of the major music publication *Billboard* persuaded the music industry to lump all popular black music under the category of Rhythm and Blues (R&B). Although *Billboard* officially changed the name in 1969 to Soul, it has still been called R&B.

A black R&B group called the Chords released a record called "Sh-Boom" in 1954. It became a hit song almost immediately on the R&B list. Within three weeks it was a top ten record on the pop charts. This was the first time that any R&B record had ever done that well in the pop rankings. The major white record companies were afraid they would begin to lose their white teenage customers to black R&B records. It had been a common record industry practice for performers to put out their own version of a popular record. It was not unusual during the 1920s and 1930s for a popular song to be recorded by over a dozen different performers. The music that came out of this covering process did not have the same feel or level of excitement as the original black version, but it was still very popular among young white teenagers. When a white group from Canada called the Crew Cuts did a cover of "Sh-Boom," it became an even bigger hit, outselling the Chords' original version.

The practice of covering was a financial disaster for black R&B artists, while at the same time it was making white artists and record companies very wealthy. White teen heartthrobs Pat Boone, Frankie Avalon, Bobby

Darin, Paul Anka, and the Everly Brothers all became famous by performing covers. The major record companies had strong promotional support, access to the best factories, and well-organized distribution networks. These companies were also supported by most of the white DJs, who would play the white covers but not the black R&B originals. White radio stations and DJs soon became major players in determining the success of nearly all recorded music. At first they would not play most popular black music because it was considered too offensive by white standards.

In addition to losing money to covering, black performers were also being cheated out of their performance and record fees by crooked white managers and record companies.

Eventually the covering craze backfired, as young white record buyers began rejecting the covers in favor of the original R&B songs. In 1956 white singer Pat Boone tried to cover Little Richard's song "Long Tall Sally." When Little Richard's song outsold Boone's version, it showed that there was widespread appeal for original black music.

"Little Richard" Penniman was one of the most famous boogie-woogie piano players. He could rightfully claim to be an original pioneer of modern rock 'n' roll music. He was born in 1935 in Macon, Georgia, where he sang gospel music in his family church. The powerful sound taken from black gospel roots helped him blast his way into music history in 1955 with a wildly delivered performance of the song "Tutti-Frutti." Little Richard's record was one of the top five hits almost six months before Elvis Presley's music began to rise on the record charts. He sang with intense energy while playing in a wild piano style that was so popular that it was imitated by others.

Elvis Presley recorded his version of several popular Little Richard songs, such as "Rip It Up" and "Long Tall Sally." It was Jerry Lee Lewis, however, who could be called "the white Little Richard." Lewis copied Richard's racing piano technique and wild, shouting song style. He also imitated Little Richard's unique stage techniques, such as standing up

Little Richard was a pioneer of rock 'n' roll and became famous with his 1955 recording "Tutti-Frutti."

while he played, frantically banging the keys, bouncing on the keyboard with his behind, and playing with his feet. Little Richard also influenced legendary black soul singers Otis Redding, Wilson Pickett, Aretha Franklin, and James Brown.

The first white singers to become famous for imitating the high-energy style of black R&B artists were probably Bill Haley and Elvis Presley. Haley's group blended hard-edged rhythms with "western swing," yodeling, and polka rhythms. After Haley and his Saddlemen sold 75,000 copies of "Rock This Joint," he changed the group's name to the Comets.

Events such as the Vietnam War and the civil rights movement marked the 1960s as a time of great political and social upheaval. The public mood influenced rock 'n' roll to move toward a more serious, softer, and socially

Bill Haley and the Comets rehearsing for a 1957 performance

conscious music. Since the music was performed mostly by white artists, rock 'n' roll became a major avenue of expression for white youth. The greatest musical influence on this movement came from a British rock 'n' roll band from Liverpool called the Beatles.

The major inspiration for the Beatles came from legendary black blues singers Leadbelly Ledbetter, Big Bill Broonzy, and Muddy Waters. The Beatles, like many other groups who came from England, were also influenced by popular white rock 'n' roll groups that came to Europe, such as Bill Haley and the Comets. It was obvious, however, that the source of the music came from African-American traditions. Performances in Europe by black singers such as Little Richard, Chuck Berry, and Chubby Checker only served to reinforce that idea.

At about this same time a revival of interest in America's folk music traditions began to take place on college campuses. The folk-rock movement included groups and singers such as the Weavers, Pete Seeger, Bob Dylan, Joan Baez, and Peter, Paul and Mary. Folk-rock performers were influ-

Chuck Berry is one of the earliest performers of rock music. His style influenced many other rock musicians.

enced by the music of black country blues singers like Leadbelly and Howlin' Wolf as well as by white American folk music. Though the music was more gentle, the words often expressed the singers' protests against the unfairness of the government and society.

In contrast to these developments, a counterculture movement known for its excessive forays into psychedelic drugs produced "acid rock." This trend was led by another British rock group, the Rolling Stones. Jimi Hendrix and his band featured music brimming with anger at "the establishment," extremely loud amplification, colorful and unusual costumes, psychedelic light shows, and drug use.

During the 1970s, some older musical styles were borrowed and others were reworked by new composers and by singers such as Roberta Flack and Donnie Hathaway. Also at this time certain rock groups—Earth, Wind and Fire, for one—tried to blend the elements of rock, jazz, pop, and classical music.

During the 1980s and well into the 1990s, Michael Jackson emerged from the Jackson Five to become a star in his own right. In order to make their music acceptable to a broader audience, black artists such as Prince,

Pop superstar Michael Jackson on his 1993 world tour

Whitney Houston holding her 1994 Grammy Award for Record of the Year

Whitney Houston, and Lionel Ritchie began a movement of African-American pop music.

Rock continues as music that has grown popular by imitating black musical styles. Publicly many rock stars give credit to the earlier black musicians. However, once an innovative idea in black music would emerge, often it would be changed in order to be better accepted by the young white majority. The idea that African-American music had to be "refined" before it would be acceptable to white American audiences was rooted in a racist perception of black cultural traditions.

RAPPING IT UP

Rap has been referred to as "the most important music to emerge in America during the 1980s and 1990s." But whether rap is spoken, chanted, or sung in that familiar and catchy rhythm, there is the feeling that rap is more than just musical entertainment.

Rap music or rap consists of a lead performer using rhymed storytelling in the street slang of urban black youth. Rapping refers to the spoken words, and rhythmic hip-hop is usually the musical accompaniment. *Hip-hop* is also the preferred term for the urban youth culture of the late 1970s with its large, portable "boom box" radios and fast-changing styles of music, fashion, dance, graffiti, and slang.

Both rap and hip-hop are often spoken of as if they were the same thing. This is a common mistake. Rap is a major element that came out of hip-hop culture. It is possible for an artist to perform in the hip-hop style and not be a rapper, like singer Montell Jordan or the group TLC.

Rap music has also been described as a "confusing and noisy element of contemporary American popular culture." Supporters of rap believe that it emphasizes what life is like in American cities from the viewpoint of blacks who live there. These people feel it is unfair for critics of rap to focus only on the most sensational lyrics while ignoring its important messages. Some say that not all rap and rappers should be put into one category because they have individual opinions. Some people praise rap as an educational tool that can be used to get bored schoolkids interested in learning. Others feel that the real-life expression of ghetto stories in rap songs helps to bring more attention to the problems of racism and economic oppression.

Opponents of rap consider it the ravings of an immoral, violence-prone, and socially unstable minority group. They believe that most rap artists enjoy shocking their audiences with graphic and obscene stories of their own self-destructive behavior. Problems they associate with rap music include violence at rap concerts, rap's graphic portrayals of cop killing and physical violence toward women, and suggestions that white people are hopelessly evil. The variety of criminal charges against rappers such as Snoop Doggy Dogg, Scarface of the Geto Boys, Dr. Dre, Queen Latifah, and the late Tupac Shakur give an image of a total disregard for the law. They also show a tendency toward violence and death at an early age. Tupac Shakur's murder in 1996 seemed to confirm the fears many have of the violent lifestyles some rappers project.

While some rappers support the other rappers' right of graphic self-expression, they admit that rap can have a negative influence on young blacks. Female rappers often strongly criticize male rappers who glorify disrespectful attitudes and violent actions toward women, while at the same time defending their right to sell their music.

Many rappers who find fault with American racial and economic discrimination also believe in personal responsibility. They support self-improvement methods based on changes in personal behavior as the permanent solution for drug abuse, crime, and family instability.

Rap music represents a tangled web of cultural, political, and social issues in modern American society. Ministers, sociologists, government leaders, and the media have begun to recognize the influence that rap is having on popular culture. According to author Nelson George, "the situation doesn't differ greatly from the one that sparked England's punk rock movement. Lower-class kids have always wanted and created their own insular [inside] thing. London youths of the mid 1970's plugged in their guitars, just as the generation before had, but said something different this time. Meanwhile in Harlem the plastic disco [artificial sound] of Studio 54 was ignored [by young urban blacks] and the music [rap] was transformed into a uniquely black and streetwise form closer to home."

Rap, like many styles of African-American music before it, may soon be more accepted by white youth and others who may share its thoughts, feelings, and daily experiences. Rap currently represents the cutting edge of youth culture all over the world.

Rap is the modern-day product of a rich oral tradition that was an important part of African culture. In African society spoken language was considered such an important part of the culture that its continuation was assigned to an entire class of male professional singers and poets called griots. The griot's job was to carry the news of wars, births, deaths, and other important events. He also had to remember the history of the tribe.

Traditional African society required everyone to understand and use language. People were given respect based on their skills in oral communication. In Africa speech was more than a highly developed art form. Efforts to use words creatively were a challenge, a competitive sport, and a hobby. It is from this background of African oral tradition that rappers like Snoop Doggy Dogg, Dr. Dre, Chuck D, Ice-T, and Naughty by Nature have come to declare themselves spokespersons for African-American youth.

Consider when a rap artist tells the audience:

Everybody say, Hey.
(Audience) Hey.
Say Ho.

(Audience) Ho .
Now scream!
(Audience screams).

Here the rap artist speaks to the audience directly and expects them to talk back. In this way, rap continues the African tradition of call-and-response.

Rap has many of the qualities of the African-American oral tradition. Concealed messages can be heard in rap similar to those found in slave folktales. Like the blues, rap can express pain and joy. Rap can be as improvisational as jazz. It can have the sharp wit and humor of professional comics and the inspiring speeches of many black leaders. Rap contains elements of the "testifyin'" found in African-American churches and the "signifyin'" comments African Americans make among themselves. It is similar to the spoken-word performances of poets like Gil Scott Heron, Amiri Baraka and Gylian Cain, David Nelson, and Felipe Luciano of the Last Poets.

Rap began in the inner-city nightclubs of the South Bronx section of New York City in the mid-1970s. It was a deliberate departure from the "brainless robotism of disco [music]." The 1970s also emphasized the overwhelming importance of radio and records as the main vehicles for the distribution of popular music. During this time the

Rapper Ice-T in performance

nationwide disco craze caused thousands of psychedelically lighted dance clubs to spring up all over America. The disc jockey (DJ) soon became an important element in the discos' success. The DJ not only played records but also functioned as the "hip-talking master-of-ceremonies (MC)." In disco the purpose of the DJ was to blend the end of one song into the beginning of the next one as smoothly as possible, hiding the breaks between songs. DJs needed long segments of music suitable for dancing and free of distracting lyrics. Long instrumental "breaks" were created from selected parts of different records, which were linked together and then taped to make even longer dance tunes.

As the popularity of disco reached a peak, a new style of dancing emerged that focused on the extended breaks in and between the songs. At these break points during the DJ's performance, dancers began to break-dance. Break-dancing became an important part of hip-hop style.

A young Jamaican immigrant known as Kool DJ Herc changed the standard routine used by disco DJs. Herc realized that the most popular part of dance music was when the singing stopped, the rhythm section dominated, and the best dancers showed their flashiest moves on the floor. Herc took two copies of the same record and put them on dual turntables. He then played the percussion break over and over by flipping the needle back to the beginning while the other record played through.

Another technique was added by Grandmaster Flash (Joseph Saddler), a DJ who had studied electronics in school. He was inspired after seeing another DJ use a switch to make the sound of both turntables come into his headphones. Flash describes what happened next: "I had to go to the raw parts shop downtown to find me a single pole double throw switch, some crazy glue to glue this part to my mixer, an external amplifier and a headphone. What I did when I had all this soldered together, I jumped for joy—[saying] I've got it, I've got it, I've got it! . . . My main objective was to take small parts of records and, at first, keep it on time, no tricks. . . . After that, I mastered punch phrasing—taking certain parts of a record where there's a vocal or drum slap or horn. I would throw it out and then bring it back, keeping the other turntable playing. . . . The crowd, they didn't understand it at first but after a while it became a thing."

Flash became famous for the way he used turntables, which were called the "wheels of steel." Although he was not a musician, he did have a talent for working with turntables and records like a skilled percussionist. At the end of his session he would play a medley of soul ballads. This mixing of musical sounds along with the rhymed "rappin'" street talk he carried on with his friends caught on. His neighborhood performances proved to be more popular than the expensive discos he competed with downtown. His rap record "The Message," became a hit in 1982.

Herc and Flash were early pioneers of rap. Their ancestors were from the Caribbean islands, where the practice of mobile DJs running their own shows was established in the 1940s. In the Caribbean the DJ was considered more of a celebrity-performer than in the United States. Most people in the islands could not afford records or record players. The radio stations were controlled by the upper classes and did not usually play music that appealed to the majority of the islands' black population. DJs soon became popular as they traveled the countryside using elaborate sound systems to play their mostly African-American and locally produced record collections.

When these DJs began to immigrate to the Bronx, they brought the technical ideas that had first been used in the Caribbean. The practice of remixing different versions of African-American soul and R&B music came from Jamaica. The DJs would prolong the favored instrumental parts and remove the vocal part so that the DJ could add his own voice. The DJ usually did not sing, but talked in a style known in the Caribbean as "toasting." Toasting was a kind of improvised oral poetry with roots that went back to the calypso singers of Trinidad and to the West African griots. Upon coming to the Americas, the calypso and African songs of praise turned into boasting. Different poets and singers competed for public recognition as masters of creatively delivered orations.

The practice of dressing outlandishly during these performances was also a Caribbean tradition. Similar to Mardi Gras in New Orleans and Car-

The rap group Arrested Development often performed in colorful African-inspired dress.

nival in Brazil, the Caribbean calypso contests included wild costumes, the use of nicknames, and mock-royal titles. All of these traditions survived to become significant elements of rap.

Rap, like the blues, is hard for many people to understand, especially middle-class blacks and whites. Much of the present resistance to the performance of rap music has come from middle-class black people. Some rappers believe this is because they do not want to be reminded of the terrible living conditions of many young urban blacks. Rappers calmly admit that they are not trying to be musically artistic, nor are they always presenting positive images in their songs about black America. Like the blues of old, rap is when "they talk about what they feel and know." The sorrow songs that used to be sung by slaves are now rapped by young people in the cities.

In an interview with *Time* magazine writer Christopher Farley, Rapper Snoop Doggy Dogg was asked what made his rapping unique. He said, "Listen to my music: it's a conversation rather than rap. Now if I'm hollering, you might turn me off." Rap, although misunderstood by many, has roots that go back to Africa. Popular rap artists continue a musical heritage that began with the talking drums of Africa.

FURTHER READING

Shaw, Arnold. *Black Popular Music in America*. New York: Schirmer Books, 1986.

Haskins, James. *Black Music in America: A History Through Its People*. New York: HarperCollins, 1987.

Rediger, Pat. *Great African Americans in Music*. New York: Crabtree Publishing, 1995.

Silverman, Jerry, compiler. Traditional Black Music Series. Broomall, Penn.: Chelsea House: *African Roots*. 1993; *Ballads*. 1995; *The Blues*. 1994; *Ragtime Song and Dance*. 1995; *Slave Songs*. 1994; *West Indian Calypso*. 1995.

FOR OLDER READERS

Awmiller, Craig. *This House on Fire: The Story of the Blues*. Danbury, Conn.: Franklin Watts, 1996.

Nelson, George. *Buppies, B-Boys, Baps and Bohos: Notes on Post-Soul Black Culture*. New York: HarperCollins, 1994.

Rennert, Richard, ed. *Jazz Stars*. Broomall, Penn.: Chelsea House, 1993.

Seymour, Gene. *Jazz: The Great American Art*. Danbury, Conn.: Franklin Watts, 1995.

Shirley, David. *Everyday I Sing the Blues: The Story of B. B. King*. Danbury, Conn.: Franklin Watts, 1995.

INDEX